W9-BBW-516

WESTMINSTER SCHOOLS

PRESENTED BY

Kevin
Abernethy
1986

SMYTHE GAMBRELL
LIBRARY

Kelly S.

SMYTHE GAMBRELL LIBRARY
WESTMINSTER ELEMENTARY SCHOOLS
1424 WEST PACES FERRY RD., N. W.
ATLANTA, GA. 30327.

A Family in Ireland

This book takes you on a trip to the tiny village
of Ballyduff, which lies beside one of the best
salmon-fishing rivers in Ireland. There you will
meet the Corcoran family. Connie Corcoran is a
fisherman and he will show you how he uses his
skill and knowledge of the waters to catch
salmon for his living. You will also discover
what the rest of the family do, what they like to
eat, and what their hobbies and interests are.

FAMILIES AROUND THE WORLD

A FAMILY IN
IRELAND

Peter Otto Jacobsen and
Preben Sejer Kristensen

The Bookwright Press
New York . 1985

Families Around the World

A Family in Australia
A Family in France
A Family in Holland
A Family in India
A Family in Ireland
A Family in Japan
A Family in Mexico

First published in the United States in 1985 by
The Bookwright Press, 387 Park Avenue South,
New York, NY 10016

First published in 1984
by Wayland (Publishers) Limited
49 Lansdowne Place, Hove
East Sussex BN3 1HF, England
© Copyright 1984 Text and photographs
Peter Otto Jacobsen and Preben Sejer Kristensen
© Copyright 1984 English-language edition
Wayland (Publishers) Limited

All rights reserved
ISBN 0-531-03826-2
Library of Congress Catalog Card Number 84-72084

Printed in Italy by G. Canale and C.S.p.A., Turin

Contents

By air to Dublin

We are flying from Liverpool to Dublin, the capital of the Republic of Ireland (or Eire in Irish). The trip takes only one hour, and as we look down on the rough waters of the Irish Sea, we are glad that we did not choose to go by ferry instead! We soon see Dublin below us, at the head of the broad sweep of Dublin Bay. We can also see the River Liffey which runs through the city. Later we will meet a man who makes his living from a river — by catching salmon.

The airport lies just outside of Dublin, so we take a bus to the city center. Dublin is a very attractive city, and has many fine buildings, squares, bridges and spacious streets, which give it its own particular character. We have a little time to look at the major sights: Dublin Castle, with its State Apartments, Trinity College, the cathedrals of Christ Church and St. Patrick's, and Phoenix Park, one of the finest public parks in the world.

The city of Dublin, like the rest of Ireland, is steeped in tradition and history. Although many of the buildings one sees in the city today date from the eighteenth century, it has a history stretching back

We see some unusual sights in Dublin's streets, such as people selling fruit from baby carriages!

Left *Trinity College, or the University of Dublin, is a major tourist attraction as well as a center of education.*

much farther, even beyond the time of the Romans.

We would like to stay longer, but we have to move on if we are to reach Ballyduff, in County Waterford, by nightfall. We hire a car, and are soon on our way down south, on a journey which will take about four hours.

Below *Ireland is a sparsely populated country, with only 3.5 million inhabitants.*

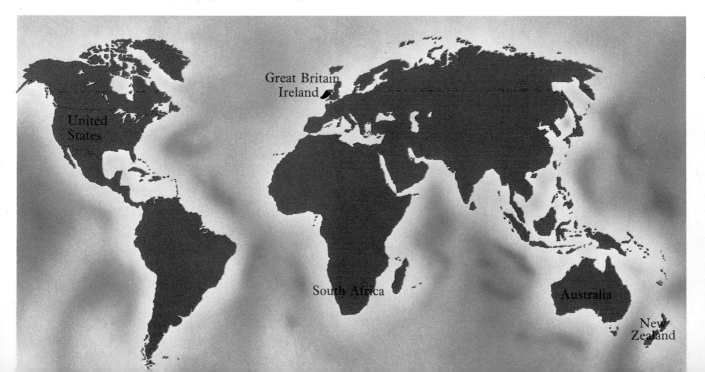

Great Britain
Ireland

United
States

South Africa

Australia

New
Zealand

Driving to Ballyduff

Ireland is a beautiful country and it attracts many tourists each year. It has a broad central plain which is ringed almost entirely by coastal highlands. There are many lakes and large areas of peat bogs. We are struck by how green the countryside is. This is the result of the high levels of rainfall and the mild climate. The lush pastures are excellent for grazing cattle or sheep. It is not surprising that about two-thirds of the country is farmland, and nearly a quarter of the working population is involved in agriculture.

The winding country road, lined with thick hedges and low stone walls, takes us through the soothing landscape of green fields backed by distant mountains.

High levels of rainfall, and a mild climate, make the Irish countryside excellent for farming.

Mountains and scenic river valleys are common features of the Irish landscape.

We notice that the signposts are written in both Irish and English. Although Irish is officially the national language, English is spoken everywhere, and there are only a few areas where Irish is the dominant tongue.

As we enter County Waterford from the north, the countryside around the Comeragh and Knockmealdown Mountains becomes more rugged, but it finally gives way to gentle grassland and scenic river valleys.

Ballyduff lies near the foot of the Knockmealdowns, beside a river rich with salmon. Like many other Irish villages, it is very small, and has a population of just four hundred. It is early evening by the time we arrive, so we rent rooms at Esther McCarthy's guest house for the night. Before we go to bed, Esther offers us some Gaelic coffee to refresh us after a long day's traveling.

The village of Ballyduff

It is seven o'clock in the morning, and we start the day with a splendid breakfast which Esther has prepared for us; cornflakes, bacon and fried eggs, toast, and tea with sugar and cream. After breakfast, we set off toward the river where we have arranged to meet Connie Corcoran.

Ballyduff is slowly coming to life around this time. The few people we see greet us with a smiling, "Good morning." It is heartening to meet people who are so friendly toward perfect strangers.

The small village stores will soon be open, and people are emerging from their houses to collect the milk which has been delivered to their doorsteps. A couple of

Signposts written in both Irish and English can be very confusing for tourists!

Above *The village stores look almost like ordinary houses from the outside.*

to the southeast coast of Ireland. It is not particularly wide, and in certain places it is only one meter (3 feet 3 inches) deep. We walk down to the river bank and see Connie Corcoran standing a little way out in the water, where it is shallow and foaming – stirred up by the whirlpools over the stony bed.

cars cross the narrow main street, followed by a single tractor. A new day has begun.

Ballyduff has seven stores in all, a restaurant, a lending library and four pubs. There is also a bank, which is open for just two and a half hours each week. The church is on the edge of the village, and from there it is only a few yards to the bridge over the beautiful River Blackwater.

The river runs for 160 kilometers (100 miles), from the hills in the southwest

Below *Ballyduff also has a free lending library.*

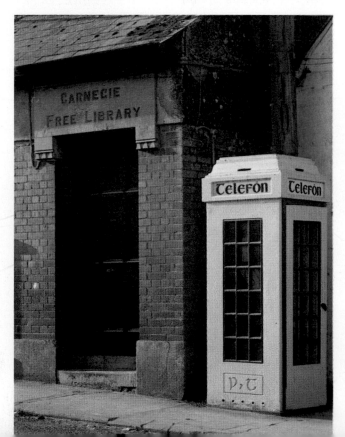

We meet Connie Corcoran

Connie greets us cheerfully. He is standing in water up to his knees, patiently watching for the salmon which pass by in the fast-flowing current. We can see that the water is much calmer just down-river from him.

Connie is 33 years old, and he makes his living fishing for salmon in the Blackwater River. He is what the Irish would call a "gillie": he catches fish for his employer, John McHugh, who is the owner of the fishing rights for this stretch of the river. John is also a passionate angler, and he often joins Connie for a day's fishing – just as he has done today.

Connie is Ballyduff's salmon expert. He can tell exactly where the fish will be, and he knows how changes in the current and water level will affect the day's catch. The Blackwater is one of the best salmon-fishing rivers in Ireland, and people come many miles – even from other countries – to fish in these waters.

Connie is paid a weekly wage by John McHugh, and his services are often hired out to other anglers so that he can give them the benefit of his experience.

Connie's services are often hired out to other anglers, to help them with their fishing.

Left *Connie Corcoran has been fishing on the river all his life: for pleasure when he was young, and now for a living.*

Fishing on the Blackwater

Ballyduff lies beside the River Blackwater in the south of Ireland, between Waterford and Cork.

It is now midday, and the sun is shining brightly above us. Connie and John cast their spinners out against the current, but the salmon are not biting. Connie says that the sun may be too bright and that they may have taken to the shade. After several more unsuccessful casts, he changes his bait from a spinner to a worm, keeping an eye on the calmer water downstream.

"When the salmon pass the quick current, they're slowed down as they enter the calm water. Then you can see slight ripples on the surface," Connie says, still watching carefully.

Almost immediately, he notices a minute change in the reflections on the water. He quickly casts out his line – he has seen the first of the salmon pass through the rapid waters, and expects more will follow soon.

Even with the strong sunlight, it is only a few minutes before there's a bite. The 3-kg. (7-lb.) salmon fights for its life, splashing with its tail and swimming up and down. But it is all in vain: after a quarter of an hour, there is one less salmon in the Blackwater.

"To catch a salmon, you have to think like a salmon. It's a question of seventy-

Above *Connie looks at his spinner and decides to use a worm instead.*

Below *John and Connie examine the catch: a 3-kg. (7-lb.) salmon.*

five percent knowledge and twenty-five percent luck," says Connie. "The weather, time of year, height of the water and strength of the current are all important factors when considering the likelihood of a catch. Then you have to decide

There's no better place than the river bank for a chat about fishing.

whether you're going to use spinners, worms or flies."

"The salmon work their way inland from the sea to lay their eggs farther upstream. Some of them manage to return to the sea, others remain in the river for a while, and a great many are caught by Connie," says John.

Connie continues: "When I have a bite, I more or less know how big the salmon is and how much of a fight it will put up. The bigger salmon make straight for the bottom, and wrap the line around stones, so that they can use their weight to break the line. The medium-sized and smaller

salmon are better fighters: they fight both on and below the surface, and attempt to snap the line with their tails."

Connie can remember when it took him a whole hour to land a fighting 14.5-kg. (32-lb.) salmon. On his fourteenth birthday, he went home with a 24.5-kg. (54-lb.) salmon – a catch he has never bettered.

"No matter how many fish one has caught, the excitement is there just the same, whenever there's a bite," he adds.

16

Even after fishing for many years, Connie still feels the same excitement when he has a bite.

Where the Corcorans live

When the day's fishing is over, and the tackle has all been packed away, we say goodbye to John McHugh and walk back towards the village. On the way, Connie tells us about his childhood.

"By the time I was 3 or 4 years old, I was already fascinated by the river. I started fishing with a twig and a piece of string, and later I played truant from school to fish. While other boys sat behind desks, I was out providing food for the family. One day John caught me fishing illegally, but to my great surprise, he offered me a job as a gillie! It made sense to him, because he knew that nothing would ever stop me from fishing here: it was my whole life."

The Corcoran family live on the outskirts of the village, in a small, whitewashed cottage which stands in the middle of about half a hectare (1 acre) of land. The land is used mainly for growing

Connie and John discuss the day's fishing, before going home.

When we arrive at the house, Jason, Owen, and Denise are waiting on the doorstep for us.

potatoes and a few other vegetables. There is also room for a goat which stands tethered in the long grass.

Connie's wife, Eileen, is 31 years old, and they have three children; Owen, aged 8, Denise, aged 6, and Jason, who is 5.

As we walk up the garden path, we see that the children are waiting on the doorstep for us. Eileen comes out of the kitchen where she has been cooking, to welcome us home. After all Connie has told us, we are not surprised to hear that Eileen is preparing the family's favorite dish – Irish Salmon!

19

Eileen Corcoran

Apart from angling, Eileen's hobbies are crocheting and dancing.

Eileen is a housewife, and she finds that her duties around the home take up most of her time. During the fishing season, Eileen is left alone during the day to look after Jason, who will not be old enough to go to school until September. She takes

Owen and Denise to school in the mornings, collects them when it is over, and gives them help with their homework if they need it.

"Besides taking care of the house, I look after the goat and the vegetables,

20

and cut the grass in the garden," Eileen says. "The village shops supply most of our needs, and with our well-stocked garden, the fish which Connie brings home and the milk from the goat, I find that I rarely have to go to the supermarkets in Fermoy, the nearest town."

The whole family enjoys fishing, Eileen included, but she also likes dancing. The Irish are known for their passion for folk music and dancing, and Eileen and Connie often go to a ceilidh in the village hall.

Her other great hobby is crocheting. This requires a lot of patience and good eyesight, but Eileen says that she finds it a very relaxing occupation. She uses fine cotton or wool for this traditional Irish homecraft.

Eileen takes the children to school each morning, and collects them when it is over.

The Corcoran children

Above *With so much land, Eileen sometimes finds it difficult to control Jason.*

Owen and Denise go to the little elementary school in the village. Classes in Irish schools are usually taught in English, except in the few Irish-speaking areas. Irish is taught as a subject in all schools.

Owen's favorite subject is history, while Denise likes the reading lessons best. When they are 11 years old, they will have to move on, either to a secondary school or to a technical school. They will have to travel quite a way to school each day, probably to Fermoy – a distance of 16 kilometers (10 miles).

Below *Denise is used to animals. Besides two cats and a goat, the family has a dog called Tiny.*

The children are very used to animals, and they look after the household pets themselves. There is a tiger-striped cat named Butch, a kitten of three months called Blackie, and Tiny the dog, who is one and a half years old.

Jason is always full of energy, and with so much land to play in, Eileen sometimes finds it difficult to control him!

Denise, like her two brothers, enjoys growing up in the country. They share

Owen loves the river, and Connie thinks he will grow up to be a gillie as well.

their parents' love of the area.

"Owen, Denise and Jason were no more than three years old when they caught their first salmon," remembers Connie. "Owen is the same as I was at his age: I'm sure he will also be a gillie. Living with nature is the only way to live."

Family life

In the combined living and dining room, Connie puts some more wood on the fire, while the children help Eileen to set the table for the evening meal. In winter, when there is no fishing, the family spends a lot of time together and they enjoy sitting in front of a cosy fire watching television. Eileen and Connie particularly enjoy nature films, while the children love the excitement of watching sports: rugby, soccer, horse racing, but especi-

The Corcoran family are devout Catholics, and attend the village church each Sunday.

ally Gaelic football and hurling. Sometimes Connie will take them to Cork to see a live match.

Religion is deeply embedded in the Irish way of life. The family goes to church together each Sunday. Connie and Eileen are Catholics, like most Irish people, and they try to bring the children up as Catholics, too.

"On St. Patrick's Day, which is on March 17th, the Irish commemorate the saint who brought Christianity to Ireland over 1,500 years ago. In the larger towns and cities, there is often a whole week of festivities, the main event being a parade through the streets. In Ballyduff, we have our own little parade, followed by a village dance in the evening," explains Eileen.

Connie thinks that such occasions are good for the village, because they bring everyone together to celebrate.

"The village is a very close-knit community, because it is so small," says Connie. "We know most people here, and, by and large, everyone gets on well with each other."

Eileen disappears into the kitchen briefly, to put the final touches to the evening meal.

The family likes to spend an evening together in front of a warm fire.

Mealtime

The food is now ready, and Eileen brings it in: baked salmon garnished with tomatoes, parsley and lemon. It is served with a seafood dressing, bread, beans, peas, carrots and potatoes. It looks and smells delicious, but before starting to eat, the family always says grace together.

During dinner, the conversation automatically turns to the day's fishing on the Blackwater. Eileen adds that it was on a walk along the riverbank that she first met Connie. For once, Connie forgot about his fishing – it was love at first sight! That was ten years ago, but they still remember it with affection.

Although they are not directly affected by the unrest in Northern Ireland and Belfast, it is a subject that is often on their minds.

"We pray in church each Sunday that it will not transfer itself down here. It's such a terrible thing," says Eileen.

Neither Connie nor Eileen is bothered by the fact that they live a long way from the attractions and conveniences of the city. They feel that the beauty of the countryside around them more than compensates for this. They want their children to grow up strong in the Catholic faith, and they hope that they will never lose their appreciation of nature.

Connie says, "We are not wealthy, but we have a rich life."

Connie asks us if we would like to visit

The family's favorite dish: Irish Salmon.

"We are not wealthy, but we have a rich life."

Left *The village has four pubs, but Connie and Eileen have their own favorite.*

the local pub for a drink before we leave. We are glad to accept his offer. The Corcorans like to do things as a family, so they are glad that the children are also welcome at the local pub – they only have soft drinks of course!

The atmosphere in the pub is warm and friendly, and we enjoy a pleasant drink while trying to convince the regular customers that we are not anglers. It is a difficult task, since most visitors to Ballyduff come because of the excellent fishing, but it is all in good humor.

Unfortunately, it is time for us to be setting off back toward Dublin again. We return to the house, and while we are saying our farewells, Eileen brings out some presents to remind us of our day with them; a piece of beautiful crochet, and two fresh salmon!

Right *The whole family is welcome in the local pub.*

Facts about Ireland

Size: The area of the Republic of Ireland is about 68,894 sq. km. (26,600 sq. mi.).

Capital city: The capital of Ireland is Dublin.

Population: There are about 3,450,000 people living in Ireland.

Language: Irish is the national language, but English is spoken everywhere. Official documents are published in both English and Irish. Although Irish is taught in schools, there are only a few areas where it is spoken in the home.

Money: The Irish pay for things in Irish pounds (punts) and pence (pighne). There are 100 pence in a pound, and one Irish pound equals about $1.12 U.S.

Religion: About 94% of the population are Roman Catholics, 3% belong to the Church of Ireland, and 1% belong to the Presbyterian Church.

Climate: The climate in Ireland is more or less the same throughout the country. Temperatures do not change a great deal from season to season; the winters are mild and the summers cool. Rain is a common feature throughout the year. The wettest areas have up to 250 days of rain, and as much as 152 cm. (60 inches) of rain each year.

Government: Ireland is a democratic republic. It was part of the United Kingdom from 1800 until 1922, when the twenty-six southern counties were granted independence. The six counties in the north remained in the UK, as Northern Ireland. Ireland has a president who is elected every seven years, and a parliament which is composed of the House of Representatives and the Senate.

Education: Irish children go to school between the ages of 6 and 15. They attend elementary schools up to the age of 11, and then move on to either secondary schools or technical schools (which provide training to prepare them for employment). Most schools are run by the state, and are free. There are also five universities in Ireland.

Agriculture: Nearly a quarter of the working population is involved in farming. The main products are meat (especially beef), dairy produce (milk, butter and cheese), livestock, cereals (wheat, barley and oats), sugar beets, potatoes and cabbage.

Industry: Ireland relies heavily on tourism. The other main industries are textiles, clothing, chemicals, machinery, food products, tobacco and metal ores.

Glossary

Ceilidh (pronounced Káy.le). An informal social occasion with singing, dancing, folk-music and storytelling.

Crochet To make a piece of needlework by intertwining and looping thread with a hooked needle.

Fly A lure for fish made from a hook decorated with feathers, tinsel etc., to resemble a fly.

Gaelic coffee coffee with Irish whisky and cream.

Gaelic football A game played between two teams of fifteen. The players are allowed to kick, handle, bounce or punch the ball. The goals are posts joined by nets at the bottom. The aim is to get the ball into the opposition's net, or between the posts above the net.

Hurling A traditional Irish game, also played between two teams of fifteen. It is played with sticks and a ball, and has similarities to both hockey and lacrosse.

Peat A thick layer of partly rotting vegetable matter, saturated with water. When dry, it is often used as fuel or fertilizer.

Spinner A fishing lure with a fin or wing which spins around when pulled through the water.

Index

Acknowledgments

All the illustrations in this book were supplied by the authors, with the exception of the following:
Bruce Coleman Ltd. (Norman Tomalin) 7, (Nicholas Devore) 8; Irish Tourist Board (Pat O'Dea) 9.
The maps on pages 7 and 14 were drawn by Bill Donohoe.